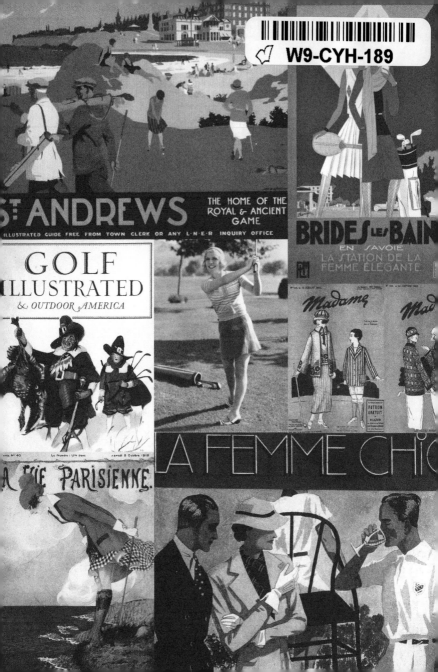

Gentlemen Only Ladies Forbidden

The Unwritten Rules of Golf

Percival Farquar

Plexus, London

Contents

To the gentlemen of the Dibden Open Club . . .
and the ladies who do not forbid them!

IT IS A GREAT TRUISM of golf that the game cannot be learnt from a book. Yet it is equally true that there are some things every golfer must know before setting foot on the course or risk the wrath of all those around him. These are things your local pro can't or won't tell you: the *unwritten* rules of golf.

After many a stroll on the links, I have gathered together the wisest counsel on the Royal and Ancient Game, and poured it into this humble little volume. Follow it carefully and, however meagre the skills bestowed upon you by nature, your etiquette will atone for a plethora of sins.

Whether you are making up a friendly foursome with your choicest cronies or entering into a vicious battle for this year's club cup, follow this guide and you will find you have the demeanour (if not the touch) of a seasoned golfer down to a tee.

If you long to hear your adversary call out in admiring tones, '*Top marks 'ol boy! Jolly good shot!*' as opposed to, in commiseration, '*I say – that's rotten bad luck, 'ol chap*' (accompanied by much smirking and rubbing of the hands) then follow my advice for, believe me, I know whereof I speak.

The ball will not always land fair; the wind will sometimes be against you and there will be times when those natty plus-fours will end the day so besmirched and bespattered by sand and undergrowth that you may have to change prior to the nineteenth – but despair not! For this book will ensure you come off with top honours even when the golfing gods are against you.

Percival Farquar

General Hints for Beginners

Tip-top tips and warnings for the golf infant

'The difference
between a good
golf shot and a
bad golf shot is
the same as the
difference between a
beautiful and a plain
woman — a matter
of millimetres.'

— Ian Fleming

Fore!

'Remember that as a beginner, even under the best of auspices, you will probably be more or less in the way of the other players on the course, and that your safety, if not your very existence as a golfer, depends very much on their *forbearance*.'

Style in the swing

'The learner who consistently misses the ball in free style, is a golfing infant of more promise than one who consistently hits it a certain wretched distance in a stiff and cramped style; albeit for the time being, the latter will always defeat the former. Do not be so scientific as to lose all dash.'

Don't be a bore!

'The friend who introduced you to the Royal and Ancient Game may indeed evince some interest in your progress, as is but proper in your father in golf, but you really must not expect every golfer of your acquaintance to listen very attentively to your detailed account of all the incidents of your first round. If you are too prolix, you must not be surprised if some of your friends hope that your first round may also be your last.'

Choose a club to suit your fancy
'Extremes should doubtless be avoided; but when we see little men with long clubs and big men with short clubs, both playing a first-class game, it is clearly useless to dictate.'

Don't try to emulate genius
'Most great golfers, and some others, have certain idiosyncrasies of manner and gesture, which are brought out in the course of playing the game but are quite unconnected with their actual method of striking the ball. Do not make it the object of your assiduous study to imitate these little tricks. It may be only in unessential particulars that your game at all resembles theirs. Genius is the gift of a few, though all can affect its eccentricities.'

Lady Luck can be a fickle mistress
'However unlucky you may be, and however pleasant a fellow your adversary, it really is not fair to expect his grief for your undeserved misfortunes to be as poignant as your own. Remember too, that it is not altogether impossible for him to have bad luck also, and that with such measure as you mete out sympathy to him, will he be likely, in turn, to show sympathy for you. I do not remember to have met any golfer who did not consider himself on the whole a remarkably unlucky one.'

Love thy golf neighbour
'Try not to forget that if your adversary should happen to get two or three holes ahead at any period of the match – even at the end – he does not thereby lose all claim to be treated as "a man and a brother". Try to remember, too, that a person may be a most indifferent golfer, and yet be a gentleman, and in some respects worthy of your esteem.'

ADVICE TO CADDIES.
You will save time by keeping your eye on the ball, not on the player.

ADDRESSING THE BALL

A golfer is a gentleman

'The true spirit of golf . . . is that of the sportsman and the gentleman who does not want to profit by his opponent's bad luck or even by his bad play, but desires to win a match by his better golf alone.'

Always tip your caddie

'If you have a poor memory and depend on your caddie to keep track of your shots, you can't expect to return a good score unless you tip him.'

Adapted from: *Hints on the Game of Golf* by Horace G. Hutchinson, 1895
'Golf Etiquette: Pertinent Pointers on How to "Laugh It Off" When Guilty of a Faux Pas' in *The American Golfer* by Sumner Witherspoon, 1922
Law of the Links: Rules, Principles and Etiquette of Golf by Hay Chapman, 1922

The Seven Cardinal Sins of Golf
For which you shall be judged, but never corrected

'You might as well praise a man for not robbing a bank as to praise him for playing by the rules.'
– Bobby Jones

1. Bending the rules (for yourself or others)
'If your ball, as you are addressing it, rolls over a quarter of an inch from contact with your club, it is as truly a stroke as the longest shot ever driven from the tee. Do not, therefore, ask your adversary "if he wants you to count that?" or coolly replace it, remarking that, "you suppose that it does not matter." If an adversary makes such an appeal to you and you have too great a regard for his feelings to insist upon your rights, you will find it a good means of rebuke, after acquiescing in his breach of the law, to make a similar error yourself shortly after, and when he requests you to put the ball back without penalty, to remark that "*you* always play the game."'

2. Holding up the game behind
'It is the duty of laggards who are not keeping their place on the green to allow speedier players to pass them whenever the aforesaid laggards have a clear hole in front of them which is not occupied.'

ON SUNDAY AFTERNOON.
She: Ned Bunkerly ought to have some respect for the Sabbath Day.
"What has he done now?"
"Why, this morning he was half an hour late at the links."

3. Unpunctuality

'Punctuality is ... a point on which too many golfers are impolitely lax. In the older centres of golf, unpunctuality at tournaments is not condoned. You are given a certain time for starting your medal round or your match, and if you are not ready when your name is called, your name is expunged and you are disqualified or defaulted then and there.'

4. Distracting your opponent

'No one should stand close to – or directly behind – the ball, move or talk when a player is making a stroke.'

5. Walking across a player's line of shot

'The real courtesy of the game of golf is that no player or his caddie should be in front of the ball in play – that is the furthest ball from the hole. It is certainly disconcerting, to say the least, to be addressing your ball with a player nonchalantly advancing either on the right or left of you and sometimes, indeed, almost in front of you.'

6. Scarring the course

Never scar the course with 'empty divots' and 'large, uncouth

footprints'. As Hutchinson so sapiently remarks, 'golf is not agriculture'.

7. Rejoicing in any shot that leaves your opponent languishing in the bunker

'Some cynical players are of the frame of mind which induced Andrew Lang to define "a good shot" as "one that lands your opponent in a bunker," and we have occasionally heard a jocular and too eager player exclaim over his partner's punishment, "hard luck – thank heaven!" . . . I once knew an opponent who stood by with a watch in hand while the

player and his caddie were looking for the ball, but this is a brutal exception to the courtesies of the game which demand that a golfer is as concerned as much for his opponent as for himself and invariably assists in the search for a ball. If there is any prolonged delay, the opponent does the graceful thing by promptly signalling to spectators asking them to assist in the search.

'No true golfer wishes to profit by his opponent's misfortune, and he will always prefer that the ball be found.'

Adapted from: *Law of the Links: Rules, Principles and Etiquette of Golf* by Hay Chapman, 1922

Little Courtesies for Navigating the Links

(Un)Gentlemanly conduct, rules to live by and the gentle art of cussing

'It is permissible to be a man while a golfer, although it is true, there is no such permission indicated either in the old or revised St Andrews' rules.'

– Cleeke Shotte

Returning 'lost' balls

'Dr Chut states that in the event of a "found" ball being claimed by its owner, the finder, instead of returning it promptly, will study it intently for several minutes and then ask in a friendly manner, "was it a Burke 30?" – or whatever brand occurs to him. When the owner, who has probably but a hazy idea as to its make, replies, "yes," the finder will remark casually, "well, this is a Wilson Success, old man," drop it in his bag and walk off. Such practices, as Dr Chut points out, are contrary to good etiquette and should never be indulged in.'

The advisability of heckling

'If your adversary is badly bunkered, there is no rule against your standing over him counting his strokes aloud, with increasing gusto as their number mounts up: but it will be a wise precaution to arm yourself with the niblick before doing so, so as to meet him on equal terms.'

"It's contrary to good Etiquette for the finder of a 'lost' ball to question its owner as to its make and then tell him casually that it isn't that brand"

A golfer never gloats

'If you have won by a revolting margin, it is polite to mark it as "one up" on the board.'

When you take the divot in the wrong place – you may say "Drat."

When you find that you have miscalculated your overhead clearance, you may say "Piffle"

When "She" appears and yanks you out of your 4-some for a mixed 2-some you may ejaculate "Gad –"

When you look for the ball in one place while it is still there in the other place, you may say "Fudge"

When you put the bunker on the green (instead of the ball) you may say "Pouff."

When a dead-straight putt halts half an inch short you may say— "Tish"

'The Gentle Art of Cussing,' taken from *Golf Illustrated*, April 1934.

Swearing on the links

'The use of American expletives on a golf course is not considered good form. Learn the names of ten Scottish champions and pronounce them rapidly when you foozle.'

Your caddie is an extension of yourself

'The penalties involved by the actions of a careless or ignorant caddie are very severe, and presumably the code was so drafted when the average caddie in Scotland was an experienced and sometimes too canny adult, instead of the half-baked lads whom too often nowadays we are forced to endure.'

On the Green

An Anthology for Golfers.

From a Drawing by Claud Lovat Fraser.

Adapted from: *Golf for the Beginner by George Fitch, 1909*
The Art of Egmontese: A Mini-Manual of Manly Manners by Guy Egmont, 1961
Hints on the Game of Golf by Horace G. Hutchinson, 1895
Law of the Links: Rules, Principles and Etiquette of Golf by Hay Chapman, 1922

GOLF CALENDAR

By Edward Penfield

Published by R H Russell

1899

Dos and Don'ts for
becoming Lord o' the Links
One must always strive to keep it classy

'I am all for golf. It has taught me patience,
persistence, determination, the futility of human effort
and several new but valued cuss words.'
– Irvin S. Cobb

Golf Don'ts for the Duffer

The following golf don'ts are by 'Niblicking,' whose putts
along the line of advice are straight for the hole.
- Don't read the rules; they interfere with your judgment.
- Don't improve your lie while your opponent is looking.
- Don't ask a two-handicap man to play with you, and
  expect him to be pleased with your game.
- Don't count a 'swing over'; it is not fair to your score.
- Don't play a bad lie; it might injure your club.
- Don't fail to blame the Green Committee for all your
  bad shots.
- Don't call your golf sticks such an ordinary name as
  clubs; 'bats' is a much snappier one.

If You Win
Don't brag about it.
Let your opponent down easy.
Let him praise the splendid game you undoubtedly put up.

IN A BUNKER.

" Dock'd in sand."—*Merchant of Venice.*

" The best kind of bunkers are natural."—*Simpson.*

If he neglects to do so, don't lose your interest in life.

When You Lose

Don't come in saying it was 'the rottenest game' you ever played. It may be, but don't say it. If you must, say it inwardly. Or retire to the seclusion of the near-by woods. There, you may release your anguish and take comfort in the knowledge that your opponent will be buying the first round at the nineteenth.

Five Laws to Lord the Links by . . .

When in peril, look to the following five cornerstones of wisdom – essential for the lordship of any links. Because blind belief can bewilder all who would battle you!

1. Waggle your way

'The preliminary "waggle," quite impossible to describe, with which golfers preface the stroke proper, is not, like the flourishes of a clerkly pen, for purposes of ornamentation merely, but is necessary for measuring the striker's distance from the ball, and for acquiring the requisite freedom and play of wrist. It is better, however, to err on the side of doing too little of this, rather than too much. Continued steadfast looking at the ball is likely to weary the eye, while exuberance of "waggle"

'One hundred years of experience has demonstrated that the game is temporary insanity practiced in a pasture.'
— Dave Kindred

tends either to the swinging of the club like a pendulum, or to slashing as of one practicing with the broadsword – strikingly effective, doubtless, to the spectator, but not conducive to the effective striking of the ball.'

2. Driving for show . . . putting for dough

'In putting, make a practice of giving the ball a chance. Extremely few putts that stop short will ever drop in. This, also, will not come naturally since the natural state upon a keen green is timidity. When in doubt, hit a trifle harder. If you will observe the situation when you are putting well, the ball is constantly coming to rest beyond the cup, not short of it.

'You should also bear in mind how, once, "the devil did grin, for his darling sin is the pride that apes humility," and that it is not altogether a wise thing to ostentatiously underrate your game. If you do so, you will be apt to raise sardonic smiles on the faces of persons whose good opinion is of more immediate consequence than that of the Prince of Darkness . . . that said, however, the only shots one can be sure of are those you have played already!'

3. The yips! That blasted saboteur . . .

'Golf is a game of controlled nerves, when well played, not of nerves unleashed. At the critical moment in many other sporting arenas one can lash on extra steam and let 'er fly. At the critical moment in golf, however, one must hold himself in even greater restraint with an iron grip upon his roistering or fluttering nervous forces unless he desires to detonate with a sudden crash,' warns Grantland Rice and, indeed, golf is a game in which mighty few of us cash in all our hopes and dreams.

4. Watch your caddie like a hawk

A decent caddie can be hard to find. But one must never settle for anything less. More than a mere vexation, the alternative can be a walking, talking blight upon your game. As Chapman notes, 'it is obvious that the responsibility attached to the caddie is onerous, apart from his helpful or distressful demeanour. A good caddie wins many a match for his principal. An indifferent or bad caddie is a serious handicap.' Should your own caddie fall into the latter category, decisive action is called for. Never forget that golf is not charity!

5. Sharp practice

The nursing of handicaps, the subtle improving of lies, the thousand-and-one other delinquencies one can commit out of sight of your opponent, are all included in the category of 'sharp practices'.

But there are other faults nearly as wretched, such as feeling depressed on a poor shot or round, complaints about an opponent's luck and one's own ill fortunes, or too much swell in the head when something fortuitous has occurred. 'Swelled Head' is, unfortunately, rather a common failing amongst young golfers, but dies with advancing years and experience.

Adapted from: *Pro and Con of Golf* by Alexander H. Revell, 1915
'Nerves, Nerves and a Better Score' in *The American Golfer* by Grantland Rice, 1920
Law of the Links: Rules, Principles and Etiquette of Golf by Hay Chapman, 1922
Hints on the Game of Golf by Horace G. Hutchinson, 1895

STYLE

Golf Style

All the gear — no idea!

'The uglier a man's legs are, the better
he plays golf. It's almost law.'
— H.G. Wells

Many a victim of the Royal and Ancient Game has found themselves drawn to the grassy fairways, mistaking them for catwalks or runways. Some may even attempt to compensate for what they lack in technical *élan* with an overstated display of (what they consider to be) sartorial *éclat*! Here are some rules of thumb for style on the links:

THE ANCIENT GAME.

'Don't take up the game as a pretext for gay attire alone … the advice of Polonius, "costly thy habit as thy purse can buy, yet, not express'd in fancy," has no application to golfers and golfines.'

'Don't wear red waistcoats on the brain, nor let plaids dominate the intellect.'

'Don't be a slave to either long or short trousers, to playing with a coat or without one, to wearing braces or a belt, shoes or boots. Be superior to the trappings of the game, and wear whatever is most convenient or comfortable. But on red letter days and bonfire nights uphold your dignity in the formal coat of the club colours.'

'Finally and most importantly: don't place fashion before comfort, nor foppishness before the score. As soon as your attire begins to overpower your swing you will know you've overstepped the mark . . .'

Adapted from: *Golf Don'ts* by H.L. Fitzpatrick, 1900

Citizens of Golf

How to identify — and where necessary
avoid — common types of golfer

'The public golf course is a great institution.
I cannot say too much in favour of it. I feel that I owe it a
debt of personal gratitude. I shall always strive to promote the
public courses. I would like to see the country filled with
them. Provided I never have to play on one.'
– John F. Wharton

The Golf Bore
'The not uncommon player who cannot go ahead until you
have changed your position to one side or the other; who
finds your shadow clouding his ball from a distance of, say,
fifty yards or thereby – and that at mid-day; whose nervous
organisation is so sensitive that your lightest remark puts him
off his game, or who complains of a tremor of earthquake if
you shake ash from your cigar.'

The Golf Pest
'Although the game is in no sense a pestilence, golfers who
are over-anxious to play when most men are otherwise
employed, who itch for the moonlit foursome, for example,
may assuredly be set down as pests. So also are those whose
only talk is of golf . . . Minor pests are, of course, as numerous
as minor poets. Among these may be mentioned men who
move too slow, men who move too fast, men who study their
putts too long and, if I were a worse man, I might include
women golfers!'

The Lion of the Links
'At every golf links there is a lion on the path of every young
golfer – a lion of the following nature:

'Whereas certain golfers, in each locality, in taking up
the game late in life, have cheerfully and patiently topped

their way through bunkers innumerable, regardless of all known rules, or, like the Cyclops of old, a law unto themselves, it has always happened that there has emerged from among the throng of these worthy men, but indifferent golfers, one who is pre-eminently unskillful. All competitors pass this unhappy wight, as he struggles in the Slough of Despond, or "bunker" in the golfers' tongue, and leave him behind them as a landmark amidst the difficulties whence they have emerged on to fair Elysian fields – a *pons asinorum* over which all have to pass before they can become golfers worthy of the name. With what joy, then, does not this poor lone golfer pounce upon the tyro, like a lion upon his prey, seeing in him a rival with whom he may cope on equal terms, possibly for years, probably for weeks, certainly almost for days! For the poor lone one we rejoice; but for the tyro it is a fearful thing. Nevertheless he must endure his fate. Keeping ever before his eyes the instructions of such a Mentor as he may be fortunate enough to find, and closing them as far as possible to the distorted style of his opponent, he must struggle over this *pons asinorum* till he has proved himself thoroughly able to surmount it, and can take his place among those who, having paid their toll, look back, as we have said, with a pity which is akin to love, upon the "bridge," as on a landmark in a portion of their accomplished journey.'

The Golf Lawyer

'The Golf Lawyer, although smaller, resembles the Common Golfer in externals, skull formation, dentition formula, etc., and is distinguished by what might be called an excessively technical disposition which is manifested in its readiness to take advantage of its opponent's failure to observe the rules of golf [. . .]

'Although naturally gregarious in instinct, the Golf Lawyer is tending to develop more and more into a solitary type due to the fact that Common Golfers, through some instinct of self preservation, make strenuous efforts to avoid him. He is distinguished by no special ornamentation,

many, in fact, having a particularly plain appearance. He is, however, remarkably thick-skinned and hardy and extremely difficult to discourage.'

The Funeral Foursome

'The Funeral Foursome is no innovation; no new discovery. It probably is as old as golf, which would run it back before Columbus came to America, and if he had got behind a Funeral Foursome he never would have made it [...] Primarily, the operations of a Funeral Foursome are based on a disregard for the feelings and rights of other golfers. They are out to play their game, so-called. If they have four-bits a corner on the match, and have to hole out every putt, and take from there to six putts a piece on each green, why that's their game. They are satisfied with it, and it's nobody else's business.'

The American Golfer

'The prevalent idea that the American is a born hustler is sadly belied on the golf links. It may be that just because he has learned to travel in express subway trains, the American has forgotten how to walk. On the golf links he walks terribly slowly [. . .] But that is not the only reason why he takes such a long time to get round the course. He takes a preliminary swing and then he waggles his club needlessly over the ball, or he crouches over it with glaring eye as if by sheer hypnotic power he would compel it to fly.'

The English Golfer

'The Englishman did not accept the game as an inheritance with all its tradition. He took it up rather as a parvenu who has purchased a house from aristocratic owners. He came in with the spirit of cricket possessing him and plays golf with less than Scottish solemnity. He is known to laugh when his adversary makes a bad stroke – he sometimes plays in flannels and takes his coat off – he often runs after the ball, frequently shouts at it and almost invariably counts his score.'

The Scottish Golfer

'The Scottish Golfer may have laid claim to this Royal & Ancient game, however, he seems unwilling to accept the mounting cost of patronage. If he is not bemoaning the rising green fees at St Andrews, he's raging on about the tide of change sweeping through

ON THE PRESIDENTIAL GOLF LINKS.
A HARD AND HOPELESS GAME FOR DAVY.

his pride and joy. There's nothing quite as scolding as the wrath of an angry Scot! Beware the links peopled with the Highland folk for it's full of peril and grunting scoundrels!'

The Japanese Golfer
'The Japanese are taking to the game like the proverbial duck to water and are tackling it with the thoroughness that is so characteristic of them. Even now the Japanese colony in London could raise a team that would give any second-class playing club something to overcome.'

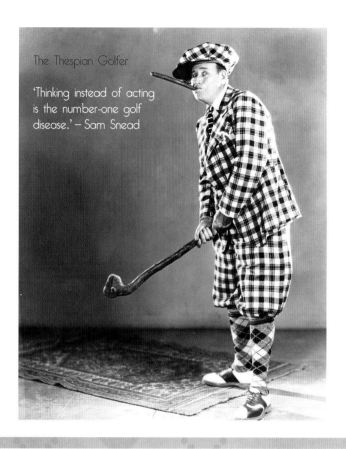

The Thespian Golfer

'Thinking instead of acting is the number-one golf disease.' – Sam Snead

Adapted from: *Hints on the Game of Golf* by Horace G. Hutchinson, 1895
'The Golf Lawyer' in *The American Golfer* by Sumner Witherspoon, 1922
'The Golden Rules of Golf' in *The American Golfer* by O.B. Keeler, 1920
'The Common Sense of Golf' in *Outing Magazine* by H.J. Whigham, 1885
Extract from *Golfing* published in *Golfing Magazine* by Horace G. Hutchinson, 1898
'British Preparations for the American Invasion' in *Golf Illustrated* by J.H. Taylor, 1921

Ladies on the Links

Beware the monstrous regiment
of women . . . (golfers)

'Selecting a putter is like selecting a wife – to each his own.'
– H.G. Wells

We will all agree that any game worth playing at all is worth playing *according to the rules*. It is easy enough to degrade any sport – however noble – by wilfully flouting such basic codes of conduct. It began with croquet in the days of our grandfathers, a game that famously fell into utter disrepute because the ladies would not play fair, passing off flagrant cheating as 'innocent enough'. Be warned, my fellow golfers, be warned . . .

Brace yourselves, boys: beware the lady of the links
'Time was when woman stood apart from golf and rated it as that which spoiled her seaside holiday by the cleavage

it made between the sexes. She adorned herself in vain, for the infatuated golfer obeyed the first of all rules and kept his eye on the ball – not on her . . . Such days as these are gone forever. Woman has best fought her case by a species of capitulation. She, too, has turned golfer, and she has won.'

Naught is fair in love and golf – and never the twain should meet

'This is a problem that confronts every married golf player. If you are not married, you are in even a worse condition, for the chances are that you have a best girl, and it is often easier to get out of playing golf with your wife than it is with your best girl. A married man becomes trained in deception; that is, if he has any genius for matrimony. With a little practice, he can easily become expert in evading a game with his wife; whereas the poor lover is absolutely at the mercy of the girl. At any moment she can drag him around the links and get him in such a condition that he may not be any good for a month. It's bad enough to be in love; but it's much worse if the girl you love also plays golf. The safest way is to fall in love with a girl who doesn't play.'

Stay vigilant: prevention is better than the cure

'Any woman is likely at any moment to become a golf fiend, even a man's wife who has hitherto been occupied solely with politics, bridge or religion. If you happen to be away from home, your best friend may step in and insist on giving your wife a few preliminary lessons. When you get back from your trip you find that the golf serpent has entered your hitherto peaceful home. Your wife is losing on the average about a dozen balls a week, and you are confronted with ruin.'

Should a man play golf with his wife?

'Your wife has become a golf player. If you don't play with her, there will be trouble. If you do, your game has gone. The cure is radical, and will take about six months, but it will pay in the end.

'Play with nobody else but your wife. Give up your game temporarily and fearlessly. And while you are doing this, offer her no advice. Be her slave. Remember, you are stooping to conquer. Tee up her ball on all occasions. If she asks you anything reply: "Yes, pet, by all means." If she makes a dub shot say: "Never mind, darling; don't be discouraged. You are doing wonderfully." If she drives about seventy-five yards and keeps in the open, exclaim: "Marvellous! Marvellous! In three months you'll outdrive every woman in the club."

It Will be Popular on the Links this Season—

THE THISTLE HAT

Non-shrinking Flexible Fibre

'Don't waver. Don't be discouraged. The operation must be complete. Surrender everything. The first thing that will happen is that you will excite the sympathy and admiration of all the other boys. This will all be silent, but nonetheless effective. And in about three weeks your wife will come around and say: "Dear old boy, I just hate to have you spend so much time on me."

'"I just love to, ducky dear," you will respond.

'"I know it's hurting your game. They told me that————"

'"As if that matters! The joy of playing with you more than makes up for—"

'She begins to look at you curiously. In another week she comes around once more and says: "Look here, my dear, there is something wrong about you. Other men don't treat their wives as you treat me."

'"Other men, I greatly fear, are very selfish. They consider their score first."

'"But you played so well before you played with me. It isn't normal."

"'What does that matter?' She grows suspicious. She looks at you queerly. She stands it for a few days more, and then—

"'I hope you won't mind, dear,' she will say, 'but I simply won't play with you today.'

"'What, not today? You are breaking my heart!'

"'Now don't be sensitive. But I am really not learning anything. You never give me any advice unless I ask it and then it isn't good. Besides, I have got to play with some one who plays better than I do, otherwise how can I learn?'

'You realize now the fatal truth. She has ruined your game. She is treating you with contempt. This is the lowest point a golfer can reach. But it is the only way to effect the cure.

"'Woman!' you exclaim. 'You are insulting me! I have

done everything for you and is this my reward?" She now sneers. The climax comes . . .

"'Why don't you burst into tears?" she hisses. "And believe me, I thought I had married a real man, instead of a weak-minded parasite who loves nothing better than to follow an ambitious woman around the links and look for lost balls. You're the laughing stock of the club, hanging on to my skirts. Henceforth you play your own feeble game and I'll play mine."

'Don't weaken at this point. You are now a free man, but don't show your joy yet. Fold your arms austerely and say in a low voice that vibrates with passion: "Very well, woman! Be it as you say. You go your way and I'll go mine. Your clubs shall no longer be my clubs nor mine yours. We are now golf strangers!"

'Muttering a few low words like this, go forth under the open sky, and, unwrapping the drapery of your shame, approach your fellow golfers and receive their preliminary congratulations with due modesty.'

Tips for the Female

Well-dressed and on her game
'Confidence and poise being the prime requisites for a good game, it follows that the woman golfer, before she starts out for the season, should pay particular attention to her outfit. To step up to the tee feeling conscious of well-cut and becoming garments is a long step towards a satisfactory score.'

On the dangers of wearing white
'In choosing a skirt there is a one thing the golfing woman should bear in mind. White may be the most attractive wear for spring and summer sports, but is it wise for golf? For tennis, there is nothing to compare with it, but one serious drawback to its suitability for a golf skirt is that it is apt to distract the eye from the ball. Keeping the eye on the ball is one of the things on which so many women come to grief, that this point should be carefully considered before one falls for the seductive attractions of one of the new white skirts. Such a little thing as this will make all the difference to one's play.'

Adapted from: *The Golf Craze: Sketches and Rhymes* by Cleeke Shotte, (pseudonym for John Hogben), 1907
'Should a Man Play Golf With His Wife (Yes *and* No)' in *The American Golfer* by Thomas L. Mason, 1920
The American Golfer, 1922

Getting Ahead in Business
How to score big on and off the links

'It has been observed that absolute
idiots play the steadiest golf.'
– Sir Walter Simpson

Golf is the most invaluable method of making contacts
anywhere in the world . . . You are with your contact for 3-8
hours at a time, away from the telephone – most important
– with a break for lunch and the attendant drinks. Possibly,
too, with a drive down and back.

HOW TO PLAY GOLF

A Book for Beginners
and others by
H. J. WHIGHAM
Amateur Golf Champion
of America, 1895-1897.

Illustrated with Seventy-Five Full-page Chronomatograph Pictures of the
Most Prominent Golfers in the Country, in Play.

Decorative Cover
$ 00.
Price, $1.50.

The book is not intended to compete at all with the classic works on the
subject, such as Badminton. But it gives in concise form suggestions and
directions for beginners and for older players, without being overburdened
with a mass of discussion and detail. It addresses itself especially to the
needs of American players, and the subjects of its many illustrations are
chosen for the most part from among them.

Order Blank.   **Cut here and forward to the Publisher.**

Herbert S. Stone & Co., Caxton Building, Chicago, Ill.
Constable Building, New York.

*For the enclosed One Dollar and Fifty Cents kindly send "How
to Play Golf" by H. J. Whigman, to the following address*

Name

City

53

You will find that the more important people you want to meet have started playing regularly after they had made their money and so are likely to have long handicaps.

If, at a four-ball, you notice that there is a very important chap playing along behind you in another match, invite him and his party to go through. Whether or not he accepts and however the rest of your party protest, it earns you splendid points.

It is very mean of you to have your name and initials stamped on your golf balls. Its end result is that if you lose one and it is found it has to be returned to you.

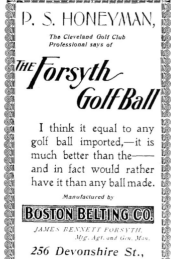

If you are playing a customer's game and he misses his first shot, say 'I always play mulligans, don't you? Have another.' (This is an American rule that means you get a free extra shot off your first tee. You could also give him three-foot putts but don't overdo it with a five footer – he may get suspicious.)

Adapted from: *The Art of Egmontese: A Mini-Manual of Manly Manners* by Guy Egmont, 1961

The Miseries of Golf

She can be a cruel and unforgiving mistress

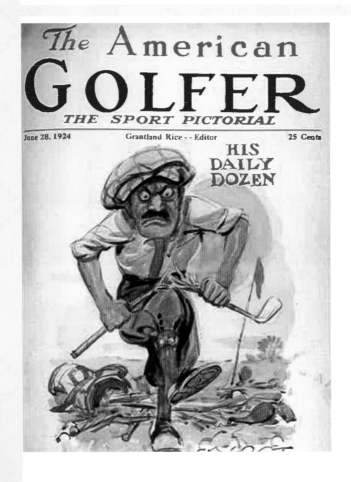

'Golf: a plague invented by the Calvinistic Scots as punishment for man's sins.'
– James Barrett Reston

That Moment When . . .

Describing in the club, at lunch-time, with great accuracy of detail, how, after a terrifically long but slightly erratic tee shot, you had the misfortune to lose your ball in the whins, and immediately having the same ball, with your initials stamped on it, returned to you by one of your audience, who had found it exactly in the line you indicated with such precision – but some fifty or sixty yards nearer the tee.

Being asked by your opponent, just as you are starting, whether you have any objection to his wife and sister-in-law walking round with you, as he wishes to introduce them to the game.

Feeling a growing conviction, as the game proceeds, that your newly inducted opponent thinks very little of it – a conviction

which is rendered no less painful by the knowledge that this low estimate is fully justified by the specimen of game which you are submitting to their criticism.

Buying a club at a fancy price from a brother golfer, and finding that you cannot play nearly as well with it in a match as you did when trying a few practise shots before it became your property . . . nor as well as this 'brother golfer' had when it was still his!

Just as you are deluding yourself into the idea that you are successfully forgetting the painful incidents of a match you have recently lost, being approached by your late opponent, in a spirit of sympathetic criticism, with the remark, 'I'll tell you where it was you lost the match' – which he proceeds to do; and continues doing long after the subject has, from your point of view, lost all its attractions.

Adapted from: *Hints on the Game of Golf* by Horace G. Hutchinson, 1895

Hints for Golfers of Riper Years

Wisdom blesses most of those
with advancing years, except of
course the 'grey' golfer

'Golf, like the measles, should be caught young,
if postponed to riper years, the results may be serious.'
– P.G. Wodehouse

I. If you lose your temper you will most likely lose the match.

II. When lying 'heavy' and undecided what club to use, bear in mind that it is better to hit the ball with the iron than to miss it with a spoon.

III. Never, if you can possibly help it, allow yourself to be beaten by a man from whom you generally win. If you do so, you are likely to find that this one particular round, which appears to you of such peculiarly little importance, is more talked of by your opponent than the score or so of matches in which you have previously defeated him.

IV. Though the henchman who carries your clubs may be a most able adviser, you will seldom, as a beginner, derive much encouragement from his criticism. If he should happen to remark, 'Ye learnt your game from Mr So-and-so, I'm thinking?' – naming the celebrated player from whom you did in fact receive your first instructions – you must not

THE GINK AND THE GOLFER

conclude too hastily, and in misconception of the Scottish idiom, that this comment is an inference from what he has observed of your play. If you should unwarily reply with too great eagerness in the affirmative, the remark which has been known to follow, 'Eh! Ye've verra little o' his style aboot ye,' will quite suffice to show you your mistake.

V. In most cases it is the loser who is so voluble in his complaints of the unconscionable time his match has been kept back by parties in front. The winner is likely to regard these little annoyances with far more resignation.

VI. Although in general you may be a most agreeable person, you will not be choosing a good occasion for making yourself particularly so if you offer to join in and play a three-ball match with two of your friends who are just starting to play a single, without any expectation of an addition to their number. They won't thank you for it.

VII. When a friend is telling you at some length of the exceptionally fine shot which he played up to the seventh hole, do not interrupt him in order to describe the even

finer one which you yourself played to the eighteenth. The merits of your stroke, possibly even of your company, may fail to meet with their due appreciation at such a moment.

VIII. Do not insult a beaten opponent by telling him, as you take his half-crown, that he is 'sure to beat you next time,' or that he 'would have beaten you easily if he had been playing his game.' He will probably reflect that if such had been your genuine opinion, it is unlikely that you would ever have started to play the match.

IX. Most men will make a better shot with the club they happen to fancy, even though it may palpably be the wrong one, than with the one, which has been put into their hands at your suggestion.

Adapted from: *Hints on the Game of Golf* by Horace G. Hutchinson, 1895

L'HOMME

Publication
provisoirement trimes
6° Année — N°
Suite du
MUSÉE DES TAILL
—fondé en 1860
MAI 194
Le Numéro... 100 F

Lingo of the Links

A glossary of terms and equipment for advancement

'Golf is a game whose aim is to hit a very small ball into an even smaller hole, with weapons singularly ill-designed for the purpose.'
– Winston Churchill

The Weapons ...

The Driver is, for the most part, used in striking the ball from the tee. In its present form, it is the evolution of generations of experiment in the direction of fitting it for that purpose. It may, however, be used at other parts of the links, if the position of the ball and other circumstances warrant. But it is not often used except for the initial stroke. It is to be noted, however, that the driver is not always used for playing from the tee and if it is not necessary or desirable to drive the ball as far as possible, some other less powerful club is used. (The **Bulger** may be either a driver or a brassie, so you will need to ask the maker for a **Bulger-Driver** or a **Bulger-Brassie**, depending on your particular requirements).

The Brassie is a very suitable club for playing long strokes through the links. It comes most into requisition when the ball is not lying clean enough to be played with the driver and when you desire to loft the ball. The club is shod with a brass sole. It has grass-cutting qualities, which make it suitable for getting at the ball when the ball is not merely on but *in* the grass. Before the introduction of the brassie, the **Long Spoon**, or **Mid-Spoon** would have been employed, but they had not the cutting edge of the brassie, hence the survival of the latter.

The Cleek, one of the iron clubs, bears the same relation to the driver that the next club, the iron, does to the brassie. It is used with a clean lie to carry the ball up to the hole, when the driver or brassie would carry it too far. It is a very useful club on all parts of the green, and is even used by some good players to putt with. It is very suitable for putting when the ball lies in any degree 'cupped' on a rough putting green.

The Iron has, much to the detriment of the links, taken the place of the **Short Spoon** or **Baffing Spoon.** Like its predecessors, it is used for carrying the ball on to the green over an intervening hazard, where the length of a brassie shot is unnecessary. It is also used in extricating the ball from certain lies. Its face is more laid back than that of the **cleek**, so that it is admirably adapted for lofting the ball over a hazard.

The Niblick is a short-headed club. The shortening of the head reflects the purpose for which it is used, that being to get the ball out of a cup, or a rut, or a sand bunker. The club is indispensable on a seaside links on account of the sand bunkers, and it would probably not be much required in an inland links. The reason of its being so serviceable in a sand bunker is that the sand does not offer so much resistance to its comparatively small surface as it would to the iron, which is the next best club to use under similar circumstances.

NIBLICK SHOTS.

"Thou can'st not hit it, my good man!"

Love's Labour Lost.

RUNNING AN APPROACH WITH THE CLERK.

"Thou hast the odds of me!"—*Titus Andronicus.*

The Mashie is a compromise between the niblick and the iron, in both its weight and the extent to which its face is laid back.

The Putter – which may be of wood or metal – is, as its name implies, used for playing strokes on the putting green to hole the ball, though it is occasionally used for running up the ball to the hole from some distance outside the putting green. It has a shorter shaft and heavier head than any of the other clubs.

Adapted from: *Drives and Puts: A Book of Golf Stories* by Walter Camp and Lilian Brooks, 1899

The Lingo ...

A

Afraid of the dark – a putt that narrowly misses the hole especially if it becomes an epidemic event in your round.
Example: *I say, Quentin, your ball seems so terribly **afraid of the dark** today. Perhaps you need to read it a bedtime story?*

Airmail – a shot that carries completely over the intended target, normally the green, in the air.
Example: *Bloody hell, Percy! I rather **airmailed** that one! Going to need a sniffer dog to retrieve it ...*

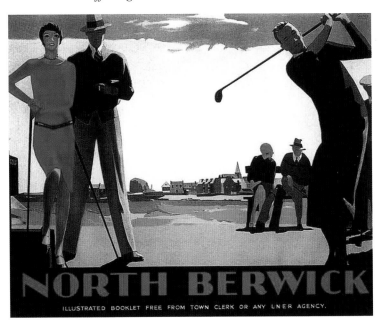

NORTH BERWICK

ILLUSTRATED BOOKLET FREE FROM TOWN CLERK OR ANY LNER AGENCY.

Albatross (double eagle) – a score of three under (less than) par for any given hole; a very rare score and thus known because of the equal rarity of sighting an albatross bird. On 8 April 1935, a day after making an albatross on the par-five fifteenth hole at Augusta in the Masters, Gene Sarazen referred to his shot as a 'dodo'. Ab Smith said his group used the phrase 'double eagle' for three under.

Example: *'Bugger! Sydney just got an **albatross** on the sixteenth,' said Cyril with a sneer. Sydney responded smugly, 'I think you'll find it's called a "dodo" ol' bean.'*

B

Backdoor – the rearmost edge of the hole from the perspective of the player.

Example: *Leaping lizards, Francis! The golf gods must be in good humour. I thought I'd missed that putt, but like your Uncle Winston, it snuck in the **backdoor**.*

Best ball – a match where an individual plays against the better ball of two, or the best ball of three. It's a common misconception that best ball entails two-man teams playing against each other, which is actually called a four-ball.

Example: *Surely we should play **best ball** today, Trixie? Given you and Flora haven't played here before.*

Birdie – meaning a score of one stroke under par on a given hole; believed to come from the nineteenth-century American slang term 'bird', meaning anything excellent. The Country Club in Atlantic City laid claim to the first use of the term. Ab Smith recounted how, in 1898/9, he and his brother, William P. Smith, and their friend George A.

Crump were playing the par-four second hole at Atlantic City. Ab Smith's second shot went within inches of the hole. Smith cried, 'That was a bird of shot,' and claimed he should get double money if he won with one under par, which was agreed. He duly holed his putt to win with one under par and the three of them thereafter referred to such a score as a 'birdie'. The Atlantic City Club date the event to 1903. (The dates attributed to Ab's reported anecdote and that put on the Atlantic City plaque vary by four to five years.)

Example: *Derek, your **birdies** are stacking up like pancakes at breakfast time!*

Bogey – is now regarded as a score of one over par for a hole. However, 'bogey' is also the name of the first stroke system, developed in England at the end of the nineteenth century. In 1890 Mr Hugh Rotherham, secretary of Coventry Golf Club, conceived the idea of standardising the number of shots at each hole that a good golfer should take, which he called the 'ground score'. During one competition Mr C. A. Wellman (possibly Major Charles Wellman) exclaimed to Dr Browne, his opponent that, 'This player of yours is a regular Bogeyman'. This was probably a reference to the eponymous subject of an Edwardian music hall song, 'Hush! Hush! Hush! Here comes the Bogeyman,' which was popular at that time. So at Yarmouth and elsewhere the ground score became known as the bogey score.

Example: *Quieten down, chaps – here comes Bertie ... the **bogey** man!*

C

Cabbage – deep rough or vegetation off the fairway.
Example: *Zounds, Bunty! My shot just sailed straight into that*

cabbage to the left. I'll need a trawl to dig that out!

Caddie (also: looper) – someone who carries a player's bag of clubs and/or assists with advice and the details of play. These fellows can be of great usefulness and service, but equally the source of much trouble. They are assiduous in offers of service which altogether disappear when engaged.

Example: *Dougal . . . when I want your opinion I'll damn well give it to you! If I wanted a debate I would ask my wife to **caddie** for me!*

AMONG WHINS.
" The shot of accident."—*Othello.*
" I have thrust myself into this maze."—*Taming the Shrew.*

Cut (also: cut shot, fade) – a shot which – for a right-handed player – curves gently from left to right.
Example: *I think this hole calls for ma' famous **cutter shot**, Fergus! Och aye, watch it fly!*

D
Dance-floor (also: green, putting green, putting surface) – the putting surface.
Example: *I say, Hamish, just hand me the putter: they're playing my song. I'll be throwing some shapes down on that **dance-floor** I fancy!*

Dormie – a match play situation where one player or team is ahead (or 'up') by the same number of holes as are remaining in the match, meaning that the other player or team can tie the match at best. They certainly cannot win.

Example: *This is an exercise in futility, Chuck. The game was* **dormie** *after the twelfth hole! I would happily hot-foot it straight to the nineteenth.*

Duffer (also: hacker) – an unskilled golfer. This unkindly term denotes approximately 85 percent of all golfers.

Example: *I'm sorry, Pendleton, but your new chum Perkins is a real* **duffer**. *He hacked his way round like some kind of scything lunatic!*

E

Eagle – a score of two under par for any given hole. Many believe this term to be an extension of the theme of birds to denote good scores, originating with birdie (see above). It would certainly be natural for American golfers to think of the eagle, which is also their national symbol. A score of two under par is, in some ways, a 'big birdie' and there's no disputing the size of an actual eagle. Ab Smith's group were quick to begin referring to a score of two under in this manner.

Example: *Eddie, that* **eagle** *came out of nowhere ol' boy. You might consider packing in the ski jumping and joining the tour.*

Even par (also: even, level, level par) – anytime one's score is level with or equivalent to par, during or at the conclusion of a round of golf.

Example: *Evelyn was really thundering through her round. She was* **even par** *until the sixteenth, then the wheels just dropped off her cart . . . it'll take some time for her concussion to subside!*

Explosion shot – a shot that removes a large amount of

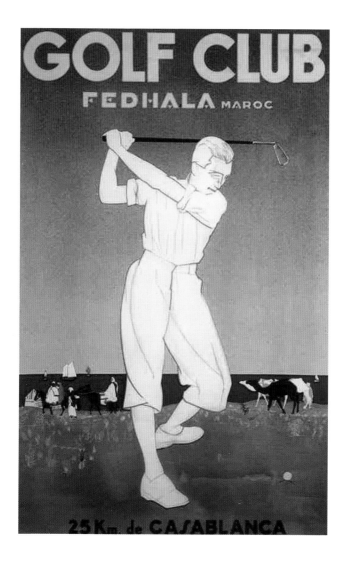

sand or earth in addition to (hopefully) the ball, as might precipitate from a buried lie in a bunker.

Example: *I tell you what, Pinkie, an **explosion shot** into the wind can leave you looking like David Hasselhoff on bad day . . .*

F

First cut – the rough of the shortest length, just off the fairway (not to be confused with primary rough, which might be a veritable jungle in comparison).

Example: *I'm sorry, Colin, but the **first cut** on this course looks like cabbage to me! It's like playing out of treacle!*

Flat stick – another name for a putter.

Example: *Old Frannie is rather handy with her **flat stick**.*

Flop shot – a soft-landing, relatively vertical shot from close to the green; usually played with a sand wedge or niblick.

Example: *My only chance at getting in earshot of the hole is to spank out a cheeky **flop shot** here – what say, caddie?*

Fore – usually bellowed as loudly as possible to warn golfers in range of the incoming flight of a ball.

Example: *'**Fore** left!' bellowed Binky as he sliced his drive savagely to the right . . . his regrettable inability to tell his right from his left was of no help to the poor fellow in the line of fire.*

G

Get up – a common command/request/plea, normally uttered in vain and heard whenever a player believes his shot will fall short of its target.

Example: *Graham was heard shouting '**get up!**' to his ball with more hope than expectation.*

Gimmie – *informal*: derived from the words 'give me,' as in 'concede the next stroke to me as holed'; a putt that is short enough in length to be certain to be holed with the next stroke. This wildly overused phenomenon (amongst the cheating contingent) is strictly forbidden in either match or medal play.
Example: '*Come on! Rollie, surely that's a **gimmie** . . .*'
'*You're not even on the green, Egbert!' replied Rollie with confusion.*

Grip it and rip it – a brash style adopted by our American brothers that inevitably gets one into trouble. Though it may work for certain *savants* in certain situations, this is widely regarded as a foolish and green way to approach any shot.
Example: '*I think I'm just going to **grip it and rip it**,' declared young master Larry as his caddie lowered his head in vanquished acceptance.*

H
Hack
1. (Also: chop) – to chop violently at the ball.
2. (Also: duffer, hacker, chop, chopper) – a usually erratic and unskilled golfer whose technique is characterised by arm-and-hand-oriented hitting at the ball, rather than a smooth swing through.
3. Unskilful and erratic golf shots or play in general.
Example: *Bloody hell, Billy, you really **hacked** your way round that back nine. It was like watching the grim reaper play!*

Halving the hole – occurs when both players/teams have succeeded in taking the same number of strokes on any given hole.

Example: *Well, Myrtle, I think all's well that ends well – we **halved the hole**.*

THAT TWO-FOOT PUTT

How a two-foot putt looks to you when you have got to make it to win the hole.

How the same putt looks when you have got two strokes to spare for the hole.

Handicap (abbreviations: hcp, hdcp. Related: handicap differential, handicap index) – the average difference between a player's scores and a set standard, as calculated by specified procedures and formulas.

Raw score – the gross or unadjusted total score for a round.

Adjusted score – the total score after Equitable Stroke Control has been applied.

Equitable Stroke Control (ESC) – maximum allowed individual hole scores to more accurately represent a player's scoring potential.

Handicap differential – the difference between adjusted scores and course difficulty.

Handicap index – adjusted average of handicap differentials to one decimal place.

Course handicap – the whole number adjustments of a handicap index for a specific course. Most courses have a chart to make this conversion. The process starts by turning raw scores into adjusted scores (per ESC) and then calculating a handicap differential for each adjusted score. Next, these differentials are factored into the formula for a handicap index. Once you have a handicap index, it can easily be converted into a specific course handicap.

Example: '*So, come on, Minty. What's your **handicap**?' asked Letty. 'My husband, Letty, my husband,' Minty replied wearily.*

I

Improved lie (also: improved lies, improving one's lie, preferred lies, winter rules, bumping it) – altering the ball's position, or the way it rests (lies) on the ground, so as to make clean contact with said ball easier; mainly put into effect when course conditions are not acceptable for playing the ball down, usually due to a wet, soggy course. One must always be wary of your opponent's desire to improve his lie unlawfully, a most common occurrence on the links.
Example: *Unless the committee has invoked winter rules on **preferred lies** without my knowing, Charlie, I suggest you put that ball back!*

Inside the leather – a distance that is closer to the hole than the length of the putter; from the head to where the grip begins. Putters used to be of uniform length and grips used to be made of leather, thus the phrase, inside (i.e. closer than) the leather (where the grip begins). Before greens were so well manicured, it was once common practice among some groups of golfers to place the head of the putter in the hole and then lay it down on the green toward the ball to see if the remaining distance was 'inside the leather'. See also, **gimme**.
Example: *Binky sportingly conceded the remaining shot after my magical chip on, as it was **inside the leather**. Jolly decent chap!*

J

Jail – when the ball is in a position where it cannot be swung at or advanced at all, in any normal way (in thick trees, for instance).

Example: *I was in **jail** on the first and I tell you, Nigel, it was downhill from there.*

Jar (also: can) – another term for the hole or cup.
Example: *Just roll that into the **jar**, Lofty, you jammy bugger!*

K

Kiltie – a tongue or flap of leather that covers the laces of some golf shoes; can also refer to the entire shoe or style thereof.
Example: *They are a jaunty pair of **kilties** you're sporting today, Kenny.*

Knee-knocker – a short putt that, for whatever reason, is challenging; the very antithesis of the gimme.
Example: *After my seamless chip from jail, Milly, I still had a real **knee-knocker** for par.*

L
Lay up – a shot played to a particular location to allow for an easier subsequent shot or to keep the ball from going too far. For example, when the fairway ends in a deep canyon and it is not possible to carry the canyon from the current position, a lay up is required – integral to good links management!
Example: *If Harry had only **laid up** on the eighteenth, the cup would surely have been his. Got too big for his breeches and now he's sobbing into his beer, poor chap.*

Like a butterfly with sore feet – a shot that lands *very* softly, usually due to high backspin and/or the altitude/landing angle of the ball.
Example: *Bart's approach on the seventeenth at St Andrews landed **like a butterfly with sore feet**.*

Local knowledge – awareness of a course's idiosyncratic playing characteristics from having traversed it many times; can often be a vital advantage in match or medal play.
Example: *Well, if it wasn't for Paddy's **local knowledge** he would never have won by such a disgusting margin . . . what a beast!*

M
Marker
1. A small, flat object – like a coin – used to mark the ball's

position (usually, but not exclusively, on the green) while other players putt and/or the ball is cleaned.

2. The person designated to record a player's score in stroke-play.

Example: *I say, Barney, would you please **mark** your ball? It's rather in my line.*

Medal play (also: stroke play) – scoring by the total number of strokes.

Example: *All I'm saying, Sally, is had we been playing **medal play** I would have soundly beaten you.*

Mulligan (also: replay, do over) – taking a second attempt at a shot when one doesn't care for the result of the first. A beginner's prerogative; not allowed in the rules of golf but usually tolerated in casual play.

Example: *Yes, Pip, I think you'd better take a **mulligan** there, unless you fancy playing your second shot from the adjoining farm.*

N

Nineteenth hole – the bar or lounge (usually in the clubhouse) to which one should always retire after a round of golf. Every golfer's favourite hole on any course; this one will never reject you or point out your shortcomings, after all.

Example: *I say, chaps, let's head to the* **nineteenth**. *She's beat us up badly today.*

O

One-putt (also: up and down) – a highly coveted event when only one putt is taken on a green to hole the ball.

Example: *I don't know if you've noticed, Nobby, but I've* **one-putted** *every hole on the back nine.*

Oscar Brown – a slang term meaning out of bounds or OB; an area that is not part of the course, in which play is not permitted – usually marked with white sticks.

Example: *Chopper hit three balls* **Oscar Brown** *then finally got his fourth attempt in play and was playing seven off the tee . . . brutal!*

Open

1. A tournament in which any eligible competitor can play – provided they qualify.

2. (Also: open clubface, open stance) – refers to the alignment of the body or clubface. For a right-handed player, the stance would be open if the body were aligned to the left of the target, while an open clubface would be aimed to the right of the target.

Example: *I was trying a big fade so I* **opened** *my stance. Perhaps* **the Open** *wasn't quite the spot to be experimenting with this, however.*

P

Par – the standard number of strokes in which a scratch player would be expected to complete a hole or course. Par is derived from a term used on the stock exchange, describing stock as being either above or below its normal – or *par* – figure.

Although the first noted use of the word 'par' in golf was in Britain and predates that of bogey, today's rating system does not. In fact, the par standard was not developed further until later. As golf developed, scores were coming down, but many old British courses did not adjust their courses or their bogey

scores, which meant good golfers and all the professionals were achieving lower than a bogey score. This meant the US had an up-to-date national standard of distances for holes, while the British bogey ratings were determined by each club and were no longer appropriate for professionals. The Americans began referring to one over par as a bogey – much to the *chagrin* of the Brits. By 1914, UK golf magazines were agitating for a ratings system similar to the US. Then came World War One (1914–18) . . . and it was not until 1925 that a Golf Union's Joint Advisory Committee of the British Isles was formed to assign Standard Scratch Scores (SSS), to golf courses in Great Britain and Ireland.

Example: *One day, Johnny, one day I'll **par** this blasted eighteenth hole! One must always live in hope!*

Peg – another term for the tee, a small wooden – or uncouth plastic nowadays – device for setting the ball up above the ground off the tee box.

Example: *Honestly, Pippy, I cannot stand the new vogue for plastic **pegs** – it's all so common.*

Postage stamp – a green with a particularly small surface area; presenting a most demanding target.

Example: *Dickie, was this course designed for Lilliputians? That green is the size of a **postage stamp**.*

Q

Quacker (also: duck hook, snap hook, snapper) – a shot that curves abruptly and severely from right to left, played by a right-hander.

Example: *Well, Quincy really **quacked** that tee shot didn't he?*

Quail high − a very low trajectory shot often used in high winds and sometimes hit inadvertently. In some disreputable circles this is also known as an ugly runner.

Example: *I say, Quentin, you really managed to duck the wind there; you were **quail high**.*

R

Rainmaker (also: skying, sky-ball, pop-up) − another term for skying the ball or hitting a pop-up, this can be intentional . . . or in most cases not.

Example: *This huge oak is blocking my route to the green, Fanny! It's time for a **rainmaker** to get me out of trouble.*

Relief

1. A rules term meaning, 'to pick up the ball and move it away from' some condition or obstacle. The rules of golf allow relief without penalty in many situations − from cart paths, ground under repair to name but a few. However, one must always ensure that relief is not granted with abandon.

2. One's emotion at finding a wooded area when bursting for the lavatory (men only − unless the woods are thick and impenetrable!)

Example: *Ah! Winnie, my ball appears to be floating in the bunker. Would you mind awfully if I took **relief**?*

Rub of the green − an accident, not caused by the player or caddie, for which there is no relief under the rules (generally associated with a bad break).

Example: *Frankly, Syd, although it is unfortunate that your ball hit a flying elephant before careering Oscar Brown, I'm afraid that's the **rub of the green**.*

S

Sandbagger – reserve this euphemistic term for any golfer who lies about their ability in order to gain an advantage in a match or wager, or turns in artificially high scores in order to inflate their handicap.

Example: *That Willy Prescott is a shameless **sandbagger** and a cad, I say! I move for his immediate removal from the club.*

Stableford – a system of scoring where a player's score is based on points earned rather than the absolute number of strokes taken:

Double bogey or above = 0 pts
Bogey = 1 pt

Par = 2 pts
Birdie = 3pts
Eagle = 4 pts
Albatross = 5 pts
Ace = 6 pts

In the International tournament on the PGA Tour they use the Modified Stableford system which is:

Par = 0 pts
Birdie = +2 pts
Eagle = +5 pts
Double eagle/albatross = +8 pts
Bogey = -1 pt
Double bogey or worse = -3 pts

The Stableford system was developed by Dr Frank Barney Gorton Stableford (1870–1959), to deter golfers from giving up on their round after just one or two bad holes.

Example: *Let's mix things up shall we, Billy?* **Stableford** *or double or quits for* **Modified Stableford***?*

Stymie

1. A term referring to another player's ball (usually on the putting green) blocking one's path to the hole – obsolete since the practice of marking the ball on the green. Sometimes by design, frequently by accident but nonetheless a very disagreeable situation to find oneself placed in.

2. General term for a situation where the desired line of play to the hole is blocked by an object or obstruction.

Example: *'Blasted Henry! You've* **stymied** *me and that was a sitter for birdie! What a beast you are!' Gerald said to himself.*

A STYMIE.
'Mark me, and do the like!' – Coriolanus

T

Tee time – the time assigned for a group to begin play on their first hole; a sacred engagement that must not be taken lightly.
Example: *Poor show, Tipi. Our **tee time** was five minutes ago. I say, that costs you at least a stroke a minute, what!*

That'll play – refers to a shot (usually off the tee) that might be less than ideal, but that is certainly good enough to proceed from without serious complications: penalty strokes, a difficult recovery, etc. The term can also be used to facetiously downplay a great shot. One rarely wants to hear the former, but aches for the latter.
Example: ***That'll play**, Virginia. All you need is a solid second shot and the flag will be in sight.*

Turkey – a little-known term for a quadruple bogey (a full four shots over par) and one you never want to hear, let alone play.

Example: *Martha made a turkey at Christmas and on the fifteenth . . .! How rapidly her festive cheer drained away as she walked to the sixteenth.*

U

Undue delay (also: slow play) – a failure to keep up with the pace of play as determined by the committee; for no good reason. To be accused of this, one of the cardinal sins of golf, is something one would wish to avoid at all costs.

Example: *Teddy took an age to read his putt, so much so that he was docked two strokes by the referee for **undue delay** – quite right too.*

Up and down – when one holes in two shots from off the green; most commonly thought of as a chip, pitch or sand shot followed by one putt, aiming one's ball 'up' onto the green and 'down' into the hole.
Example: *Jocinta may have airmailed her second shot past the green, but remarkably got **up and down** for birdie.*

V

Vardon grip (also: overlap grip, overlapping grip) – the most common grip in use today, named after historic player Harry Vardon. In this hold, the baby finger of the lower hand overlaps and rests on the index finger, or between the index and middle fingers, of the upper hand.
Example: *Old Ginty McGee uses the **Vardon grip**, but I could never quite get on with it!*

W

Whiff shot – a swing with intent to strike the ball followed by a clean miss of ball and earth.
Example: *According to Humphrey, a **whiff shot** counts as stroke, you know?*

Worm-burner – a shot with such a low trajectory that it appears to, or actually does, skim the ground; not necessarily ineffective but almost certainly unintentional.
Example: *Wendy, that was a hell of a **worm-burner**! Still, she'll play . . .*

Y

Yank (also: pull, jerk) – a shot that goes severely to the left of the target line, as played by a right-hander. Example: *I give up, Percy. If I'm not shanking it, I'm **yanking** it! And there is no happy ending.*

You can't paint pictures on a scorecard – a consolatory term, often used to appease those responsible for such ugly shots such as the worm-burner, the point being that what the shot lacks in aesthetic merit, it makes up for in distance. Example: *By Jove, Cybil! That shot may be as pretty as your dearly departed mother but **you can't paint pictures on a scorecard** – chin up!*

Z

Zinger – normally a tee shot, but also applicable to a long iron that carries further than the average shot; either way, the zinger is something to be treasured. Example: *Pippin must have had his porridge oats this morning; he hit a **zinger** on the twelfth that travelled like it was on jet fuel!*

Percival's Library

A bibliography: to be consumed with a cigar and a fine brandy

Books

Hints on the Game of Golf by Horace G. Hutchinson, 1895

Law of the Links: Rules, Principles and Etiquette of Golf by Hay Chapman, 1922

Golf for the Beginner by George Fitch, 1909

The Art of Egmontese: A Mini-Manual of Manly Manners by Guy Egmont, 1961

Pro and Con of Golf, by Alexander H. Revell, 1915

Golf Don'ts by H.L. Fitzpatrick, 1900

An ABC of Golf by D.W.C. Falls, 1898

Drives and Puts: A Book of Golf Stories by Walter Camp and Lilian Brooks, 1899

The Golf Craze: Sketches and Rhymes by Cleeke Shotte, (pseudonym for John Hogben), 1907

The Winning Shot by Jerome D. Travers and Grantland Rice, 1915

Golfing by Horace G. Hutchinson, 1898

Fore! Life's Book for Golfers by *Life* Publishing Co., 1900

L'affiche de golf by Alexis Orloff, 2002

Articles

'Nerves, Nerves and a Better Score' in *The American Golfer* (periodical), by Grantland Rice, 1920

'Golf Etiquette: Pertinent Pointers on How to "Laugh It Off" When Guilty of a Faux Pas' in *The American Golfer* (periodical) by Sumner Witherspoon, 1922

'The Golf Lawyer' in *The American Golfer* (periodical) by Sumner Witherspoon, 1922

'The Golden Rules of Golf' in *The American Golfer* (periodical) by O.B. Keeler, 1920

'The Common Sense of Golf' in *Outing Magazine* by H.J. Whigham, 1885

'British Preparations for the American Invasion' in *Golf Illustrated* (magazine) by J.H. Taylor, 1921

'Should a Man Play Golf With His Wife (Yes *and* No)' in *The American Golfer* (periodical) by Thomas L. Mason, 1920

All rights reserved including the right of
reproduction in whole or in part in any form
First published in 2016
by Plexus Publishing Limited
Copyright © 2016
by Plexus Publishing Limited
Published by Plexus Publishing Limited
The Studio, Hillgate Place
18-20 Balham Hill
London SW12 9ER
www.plexusbooks.com

British Library Cataloguing in Publication Data
A catalogue record for this book is available from
the British Library

ISBN-13: 978-0-85965-527-9

Book and cover design by Coco Balderrama
Printed in Europe by Imago

Acknowledgements

Gentlemen Only Ladies Forbidden assembles
writing from an eclectic array of vintage books,
journals, periodicals and magazines. Professional
thanks are due to the authors of: *Hints on the
Game of Golf*, Horace G. Hutchinson, 1895; 'Golf
Etiquette: Pertinent Pointers on How to "Laugh
It Off" When Guilty of a Faux Pas', Sumner
Witherspoon, *The American Golfer*, 1922; *Law
of the Links: Rules, Principles and Etiquette of
Golf*, Hay Chapman, 1922; *Golf for the Beginner*,
George Fitch, 1909; *The Art of Egmontese: A
Mini-Manual of Manly Manners*, Guy Egmont,
1961; *Pro and Con of Golf*, Alexander H. Revell,
1915; 'Nerves, Nerves and a Better Score',
Grantland Rice, *The American Golfer*, 1920; *Golf
Don'ts*, H.L. Fitzpatrick, 1900; *Golf Illustrated*,
1934; *The Golfer*, 1897; *The American Annual Golf
Guide*, 1916; *Harper's Official Golf Guide*, 1916;

Drives and Puts: A Book of Golf Stories, Walter
Camp and Lilian Brooks, 1899; *An ABC of Golf*,
D.W.C. Falls, 1898; *The Winning Shot*, Jerome D.
Travers and Grantland Rice, 1915; the *Manchester
Guardian*; the *Nebraska Star*, Edgar A. Guest,
1930; 'The Golfer's Paradise', *Pall Mall Gazette*,
1884; 'The Golf Lawyer', Sumner Witherspoon,
The American Golfer, 1922; 'The Golden Rules
of Golf', O.B. Keeler, *The American Golfer*, 1920;
'The Common Sense of Golf', H.J. Whigham,
Outing Magazine, 1885; *Golfing Magazine*, 1898;
'British Preparations for the American Invasion',
J.H. Taylor, *Golf Illustrated*, 1921; *The Golf Craze:
Sketches and Rhymes*, Cleeke Shotte/John Hogben,
1907; 'Should a Man Play Golf With His Wife
(Yes and No)', Thomas L. Mason, *The American
Golfer*, 1920; *Golfing*, Horace G. Hutchinson,
1898; *Fore! Life's Book for Golfers*, *Life* Publishing
Co., 1900; 'The Golfer's Paradise', the *Pall Mall
Gazette*, 1884; 'A Defiance', Anonymous, *The
American Golfer*, 1922; 'The Smithy of the Links',
Anonymous, the *Manchester Guardian*; 'Battling
with Bogey: A Golfer', James Francis Burke, *The
American Golfer*; 'A Lay of the Links', Sir Arthur
Conan Doyle, 1893; 'Funeral Poem for a Golfer',
Edgar A. Guest, the *Nebraska Star*, *L'affiche de golf*,
Alexis Orloff, 2002.

The following websites and online archives
have also been invaluable: babel.hathitrust.org,
UNZ.org, library.la84.org, usga.org, usgamuseum.
com, loc.gov.

It has not always been possible to trace
copyright sources and the publisher would be glad to
hear from any unacknowledged copyright holders.

We would like to thank the following for
supplying images: rjh/Shutterstock; VKA/
Shutterstock; Library of Congress; Graphic
Artists/Getty Images; The *Golfer's Alphabet*;
Fore! Life's Book for Golfers; Popperfoto/Getty
Images; Topical Press Agency/Getty Images;
Transcendental Graphics/Getty Images; *Golf
Illustrated*; *Pen and Pencil Sketches on the Game of
Golf*; Everett Collection/Shutterstock; *Golf Yarns:
The Best Things About the Game of Golf*; Stock
Montage/Getty Images; E. Bacon/Stringer/Getty
Images; Harris and Ewing Collection; Three
Lions/Stringer/Getty Images; *The American
Annual Golf Guide*, *The Golfer*; *Harper's Weekly*;
Heritage Images/Hulton Archive/Getty Images.